THE FUTURE OF HUMANITY: NAVIGATING TECHNOLOGICAL ADVANCEMENTS AND GLOBAL CHALLENGES.

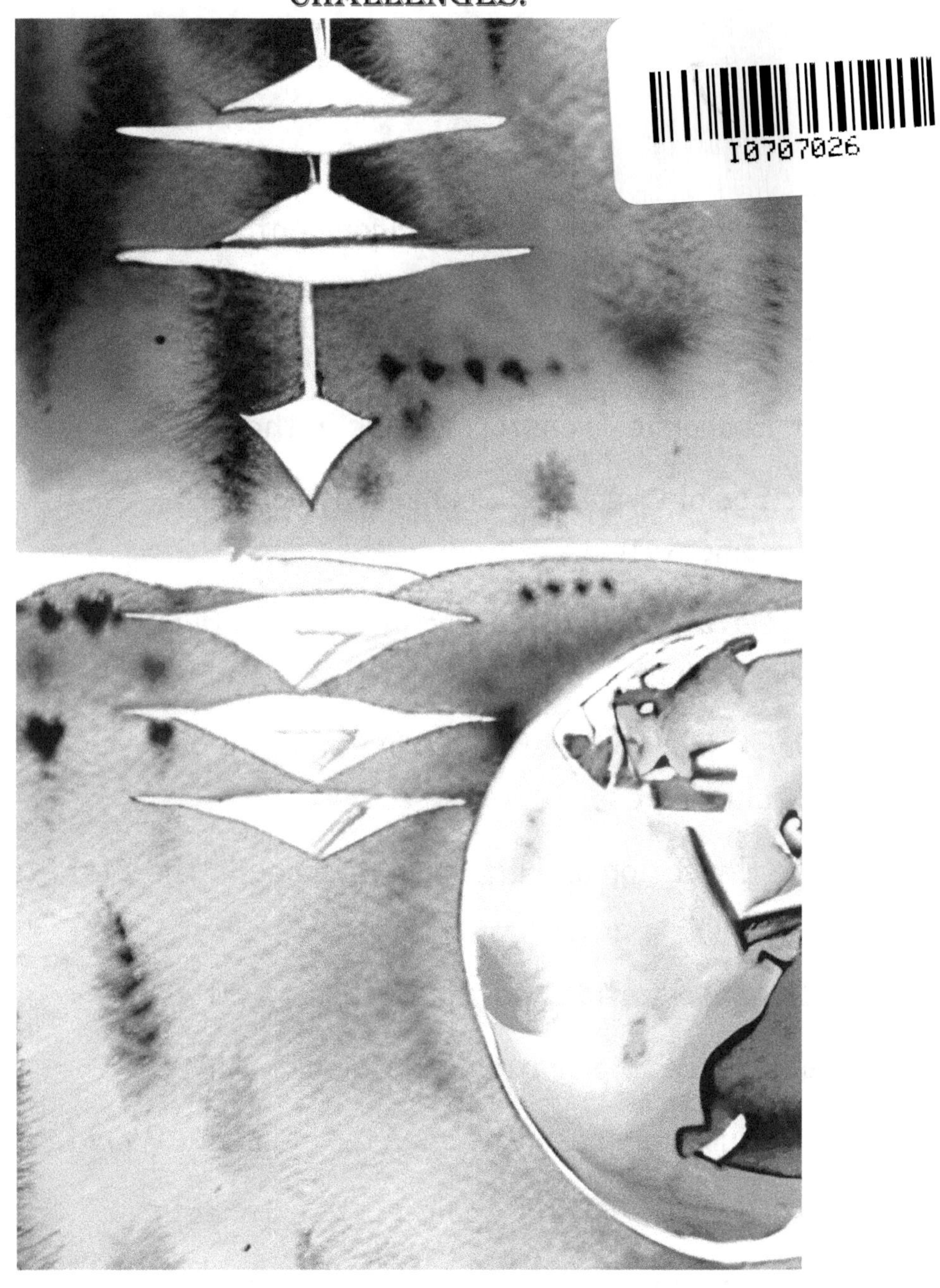

I0707026

CHAPTER LIST:

1. The Technological Landscape

2. Artificial Intelligence and Its Implications for Society

3. Sustainable Development Goals

4. Climate Change and Environmental Sustainability

5. Global Health Challenges and Innovations

6. Economic Transformations in the Digital Age

7. Social Dynamics: Connectivity and Fragmentation

8. Governance in the Era of Technological Disruption

9. Ethical Considerations in Emerging Technologies

10. Education and Lifelong Learning in the 21st Century

11. Urbanization and the Future of Cities

12. Space Exploration and Colonization

13. Cultural Preservation in a Globalized World

14. Security in the Age of Cyber Threats

15. Personal Well-being in an Interconnected World

BOOK INTRODUCTION

In "The Future of Humanity: Navigating Technological Advancements and Global Challenges," we embark on a journey to explore the intricate interplay between technology, society, and the planet. As we stand at the precipice of a new era marked by unprecedented technological advancements and complex global challenges, it has become increasingly imperative to chart a course towards a sustainable and prosperous future for humanity.

This book delves into the multifaceted landscape of the future, examining key themes such as artificial intelligence, sustainable development, climate change, global health, and economic transformation. Through in-depth analysis and insightful commentary, we aim to equip readers with the knowledge and tools necessary to navigate the complexities of our rapidly evolving world.

Each chapter offers a comprehensive exploration of its respective topic, drawing upon the latest research, expert opinions, and real-world examples to provide a holistic understanding of the challenges and opportunities that lie ahead. From the ethical considerations of emerging technologies to the implications of urbanization and space exploration, "The Future of Humanity" offers a thought-provoking examination of the forces shaping our collective destiny.

As we confront the uncertainties of the future, it is essential to approach these challenges with foresight, empathy, and a commitment to fostering positive change. Through collaboration, innovation, and informed decision-making, we can steer humanity towards a future defined by progress, resilience, and shared prosperity.

CHAPTER 1

THE TECHNOLOGICAL LANDSCAPE: PAST, PRESENT, AND FUTURE

The journey of humanity through time has been intricately intertwined with technological advancements. From the discovery of fire to the invention of the wheel, each innovation has shaped the course of history, propelling us towards new frontiers of knowledge and progress. In this chapter, we embark on a retrospective exploration of the technological landscape, tracing its evolution from ancient civilizations to the digital age and beyond.

The story of human ingenuity is one of continuous innovation and adaptation. Millennia ago, our ancestors harnessed the power of tools and agriculture, laying the foundation for settled societies and the rise of civilizations. The invention of writing enabled the preservation and dissemination of knowledge, paving the way for cultural exchange and intellectual growth. Over time, advancements in engineering, metallurgy, and navigation expanded the horizons of exploration and trade, connecting distant lands and cultures in a global exchange of goods and ideas.

The Industrial Revolution marked a pivotal turning point in human history, ushering in an era of mechanization and mass production. Steam engines, electricity, and the assembly line revolutionized manufacturing, leading to unprecedented economic growth and urbanization. The 20th century witnessed the dawn of the Information Age, characterized by rapid advancements in computing, telecommunications, and the internet. The emergence of digital technologies transformed every aspect of society, from communication and commerce to entertainment and education.

As we stand on the cusp of the Fourth Industrial Revolution, characterized by the convergence of digital, biological, and physical technologies, the pace of innovation shows no signs of slowing down. Artificial intelligence, blockchain, biotechnology, and quantum computing are poised to reshape industries, redefine work and leisure, and fundamentally alter the fabric of society. The proliferation of smart devices, interconnected systems, and big data heralds the dawn of a hyperconnected world, where information flows freely across borders and boundaries.

However, alongside the promise of progress, technological advancements also raise profound questions and concerns. The growing digital divide threatens to exacerbate inequalities, leaving marginalized communities behind in the march towards prosperity. Cybersecurity threats loom large in an era of interconnectedness, posing risks to personal privacy, national security, and the stability of critical infrastructure. Ethical dilemmas surrounding artificial intelligence, autonomous weapons, and genetic engineering demand careful consideration and responsible stewardship.

As we navigate the complex terrain of the technological landscape, it is essential to approach innovation with mindfulness and foresight. By harnessing the power of technology for the greater good, we can unlock new opportunities for human flourishing, empower individuals and communities, and build a future that is equitable, inclusive, and sustainable.

CHAPTER 2

ARTIFICIAL INTELLIGENCE AND ITS IMPLICATIONS FOR SOCIETY

Artificial Intelligence (AI) stands as one of the most transformative technologies of the 21st century, promising to revolutionize industries, reshape economies, and redefine the very fabric of society. In this chapter, we delve into the multifaceted landscape of AI, exploring its applications, implications, and ethical considerations in a world increasingly driven by data and algorithms.

The dawn of AI can be traced back to the birth of computer science and the pioneering work of visionaries such as Alan Turing and John McCarthy. Early AI systems focused on rule-based reasoning and symbolic manipulation, laying the groundwork for the development of expert systems and decision-support tools in fields ranging from medicine to finance. However, progress remained incremental until the advent of machine learning and neural networks, which unlocked new frontiers of AI by enabling computers to learn from vast amounts of data and improve their performance over time.

Today, AI permeates every aspect of our lives, from personalized recommendations on streaming platforms to autonomous vehicles navigating city streets. Natural language processing enables virtual assistants like Siri and Alexa to understand and respond to human speech, while computer vision powers facial recognition systems and automated surveillance. In healthcare, AI algorithms analyse medical images and patient data to assist clinicians in diagnosis and treatment planning, offering the potential to improve outcomes and reduce costs.

The rise of AI holds immense promise for enhancing productivity, driving innovation, and addressing some of the most pressing challenges facing humanity, from healthcare and education to climate change and poverty alleviation. Machine learning algorithms are being deployed to optimize energy consumption, predict natural disasters, and accelerate drug discovery, empowering scientists and policymakers with powerful tools for decision-making and problem-solving.

However, the proliferation of AI also raises profound questions and concerns about its societal impact and ethical implications. As AI systems become increasingly autonomous and complex, issues surrounding transparency, accountability, and bias come to the forefront. The use of AI in decision-making processes, such as hiring, lending, and criminal justice, has sparked debates about fairness, equity, and due process. Algorithmic biases, ingrained in training data and perpetuated by flawed models, have led to instances of discrimination and injustice, highlighting the need for greater diversity, equity, and inclusion in AI development and deployment.

Moreover, the rise of AI poses existential risks to the future of work, as automation threatens to displace millions of jobs and exacerbate inequalities. While AI has the potential to create new opportunities and industries, it also poses challenges in terms of workforce reskilling, social safety nets, and economic transition. Addressing these challenges requires a comprehensive approach that combines technological innovation with policy intervention, lifelong learning, and social dialogue.

In navigating the complex landscape of AI, it is essential to strike a balance between innovation and responsibility, harnessing the power of AI to benefit society while mitigating its risks and unintended consequences. By fostering interdisciplinary collaboration, ethical oversight, and public engagement, we can ensure that AI remains a force for good, advancing human welfare and promoting shared prosperity in the decades to come.

CHAPTER 3

SUSTAINABLE DEVELOPMENT GOALS: BUILDING A BETTER FUTURE

In the face of mounting global challenges such as climate change, biodiversity loss, and social inequality, the Sustainable Development Goals (SDGs) stand as a beacon of hope for a more equitable and sustainable future. In this chapter, we explore the origins, significance, and implementation of the SDGs, highlighting their role in addressing pressing environmental, social, and economic issues on a global scale.

The SDGs, adopted by all United Nations Member States in 2015, represent a universal call to action to end poverty, protect the planet, and ensure prosperity for all by 2030. Comprising 17 interlinked goals and 169 targets, the SDGs provide a comprehensive framework for sustainable development, addressing a wide range of issues including poverty, hunger, health, education, gender equality, clean water, affordable and clean energy, decent work, industry innovation and infrastructure, reduced inequalities, sustainable cities and communities, responsible consumption and production, climate action, life below water, life on land, peace, justice, and strong institutions, and partnerships for the goals.

At the heart of the SDGs is the principle of leaving no one behind, recognizing the interconnectedness of social, economic, and environmental issues and the need for integrated and holistic approaches to development. By addressing the root causes of poverty and inequality, promoting inclusive and sustainable economic growth, and protecting the planet's natural resources, the SDGs aim to create a world where all people can thrive in harmony with nature.

The implementation of the SDGs requires concerted efforts and collaboration at all levels, from governments and international organizations to civil society, the private sector, and individuals. Progress towards the goals is measured through a set of global indicators, which track key metrics such as poverty rates, access to education and healthcare, carbon emissions, and biodiversity loss. While significant strides have been made since the adoption of the SDGs, much remains to be done to achieve their ambitious targets by 2030.

One of the key challenges in advancing the SDGs is mobilizing the necessary resources and political will to drive transformative change. This requires innovative financing mechanisms, technology transfer, capacity building, and international cooperation to support developing countries in their pursuit of sustainable development. It also entails reimagining economic systems and consumption patterns to prioritize human well-being and environmental stewardship over short-term profits.

Central to the success of the SDGs is the engagement and empowerment of local communities, marginalized groups, and future generations in the decision-making process. By ensuring participatory and inclusive governance, fostering education and awareness, and promoting gender equality and social justice, we can build resilient and sustainable societies that are capable of weathering the challenges of the 21st century.

As we strive to build a better future for all, the SDGs serve as a roadmap for collective action and transformative change. By embracing the principles of sustainability, equity, and solidarity, we can chart a course towards a world where every person has the opportunity to live a life of dignity and fulfilment, and where the planet thrives for generations to come.

CHAPTER 4

CLIMATE CHANGE AND ENVIRONMENTAL SUSTAINABILITY

Climate change represents one of the most pressing challenges of our time, with far-reaching implications for the environment, economy, and society. In this chapter, we delve into the science of climate change, its causes and impacts, and the urgent need for global action to mitigate its effects and build a more sustainable future.

The Earth's climate has undergone significant changes throughout its history, driven by natural factors such as volcanic eruptions, variations in solar radiation, and changes in the Earth's orbit. However, the current warming trend is unprecedented in both its speed and scale, largely attributed to human activities such as the burning of fossil fuels, deforestation, and industrial processes that release greenhouse gases into the atmosphere.

The consequences of climate change are already being felt around the world, from rising temperatures and sea levels to more frequent and severe extreme weather events such as hurricanes, droughts, and wildfires. These changes pose grave risks to ecosystems, biodiversity, and human well-being, threatening food and water security, displacing populations, and exacerbating social and economic inequalities.

Mitigating climate change requires urgent and concerted efforts to reduce greenhouse gas emissions and transition to a low-carbon economy. This involves phasing out fossil fuels in favour of renewable energy sources such as solar, wind, and hydroelectric power, improving energy efficiency in buildings, transportation, and industry, and adopting sustainable land-use practices that preserve forests and ecosystems.

In addition to mitigation, adaptation measures are also needed to build resilience to the impacts of climate change and protect vulnerable communities and ecosystems. This includes investing in infrastructure that can withstand extreme weather events, implementing early warning systems for natural disasters, and promoting nature-based solutions such as reforestation and wetland restoration to enhance ecosystem resilience.

Addressing climate change requires international cooperation and solidarity, as it is a global problem that transcends national borders and interests. The Paris Agreement, adopted in 2015 by nearly 200 countries, represents a landmark accord in the fight against climate change, setting ambitious targets to limit global warming to well below 2 degrees Celsius above pre-industrial levels and pursuing efforts to limit it to 1.5 degrees Celsius.

However, achieving these goals will require unprecedented levels of ambition and commitment from governments, businesses, and civil society. It will also require mobilizing resources to support developing countries in their transition to low-carbon, climate-resilient economies and ensuring that the benefits of climate action are equitably distributed among all segments of society.

Ultimately, addressing climate change is not only a matter of environmental stewardship but also one of social justice and intergenerational equity. By taking decisive action to reduce emissions, protect ecosystems, and build resilience, we can safeguard the planet for future generations and create a more sustainable and prosperous world for all.

CHAPTER 5
GLOBAL HEALTH CHALLENGES & INNOVATIONS

Health is a fundamental human right, yet millions around the world lack access to essential healthcare services, face preventable diseases, and suffer from inadequate sanitation and nutrition. In this chapter, we examine the complex landscape of global health challenges, exploring the root causes of disease burden, disparities in healthcare access, and innovative solutions to promote health equity and well-being for all.

At the heart of global health challenges lie a myriad of interconnected factors, including poverty, lack of education, inadequate sanitation, and limited access to healthcare services. Infectious diseases such as malaria, tuberculosis, and HIV/AIDS continue to ravage communities in low- and middle-income countries, claiming millions of lives each year and placing immense strain on fragile health systems.

Moreover, non-communicable diseases (NCDs) such as heart disease, cancer, and diabetes are on the rise, fuelled by changing lifestyles, urbanization, and environmental factors. These diseases not only contribute to premature mortality and disability but also impose a significant economic burden on individuals, families, and societies, perpetuating the cycle of poverty and inequality.

Addressing global health challenges requires a comprehensive and integrated approach that addresses the social, economic, and environmental determinants of health. This includes investing in primary healthcare infrastructure, strengthening health systems, and promoting disease prevention and health promotion strategies at the community level.

In recent years, technological innovations have emerged as powerful tools for improving healthcare access, delivery, and outcomes. Telemedicine, for example, enables patients to consult with healthcare providers remotely, expanding access to specialized care in underserved areas. Mobile health (mHealth) applications empower individuals to monitor their health, track diseases, and access health information and services through their smartphones.

Advancements in medical technology, such as genomics, precision medicine, and regenerative therapies, hold promise for revolutionizing diagnosis and treatment approaches, offering personalized and targeted interventions for a wide range of diseases. Meanwhile, artificial intelligence and machine learning are being deployed to analyse vast amounts of healthcare data, identify patterns and trends, and support clinical decision-making processes.

However, realizing the full potential of health innovations requires addressing barriers such as affordability, accessibility, and regulatory challenges. Inequities in access to healthcare technologies must be addressed to ensure that all individuals, regardless of their socioeconomic status or geographic location, can benefit from the latest advancements in medical science.

Furthermore, fostering global collaboration and solidarity is essential for addressing emerging health threats such as pandemics and antimicrobial resistance. The COVID-19 pandemic, in particular, has underscored the interconnectedness of health security and the need for coordinated action to prevent, detect, and respond to infectious disease outbreaks on a global scale.

In conclusion, addressing global health challenges requires a multifaceted approach that combines efforts to strengthen health systems, promote disease prevention, and harness the power of innovation and technology. By working together to tackle the root causes of poor health and inequity, we can create a world where everyone has the opportunity to lead a healthy and fulfilling life.

CHAPTER 6
ECONOMIC TRANSFORMATIONS IN THE DIGITAL AGE

The digital age has brought about profound transformations in the global economy, reshaping industries, labour markets, and business models in unprecedented ways. In this chapter, we explore the impact of digital technologies on economic growth, employment patterns, and income distribution, as well as the opportunities and challenges they present for policymakers, businesses, and workers alike.

The advent of digital technologies such as the internet, mobile devices, and cloud computing has ushered in a new era of connectivity, enabling instant communication, collaboration, and commerce on a global scale. E-commerce platforms have democratized access to markets, allowing businesses of all sizes to reach customers around the world and disrupting traditional retail models. The gig economy has emerged as a new form of employment, offering flexibility and autonomy to workers while also raising concerns about job security and labour rights.

At the same time, digital technologies have fuelled productivity gains and innovation across industries, driving economic growth and prosperity. Automation and artificial intelligence have streamlined business processes, increased efficiency, and unlocked new opportunities for value creation. Digital platforms and marketplaces have created new avenues for entrepreneurship and wealth generation, empowering individuals to monetize their skills and assets in innovative ways.

However, the benefits of digital transformation have not been evenly distributed, leading to widening disparities in income, wealth, and opportunity. The rise of digital monopolies and platform economies has concentrated wealth and power in the hands of a few tech giants, exacerbating market concentration and stifling competition. Meanwhile, concerns have been raised about the precariousness of gig work, with many workers facing low wages, unpredictable hours, and limited access to benefits such as healthcare and retirement savings.

Moreover, digital technologies have also raised ethical and regulatory challenges, particularly in areas such as data privacy, cybersecurity, and antitrust enforcement. The proliferation of personal data collected by tech companies has raised concerns about privacy and surveillance, prompting calls for stricter regulations to protect consumer rights and mitigate the risks of data breaches and misuse. Antitrust authorities are grappling with the market dominance of tech giants and the implications for competition, innovation, and consumer welfare in digital markets.

Addressing these challenges requires a coordinated and holistic approach that balances innovation with regulation, competition with consumer protection, and economic growth with social inclusion. Policymakers must ensure that the benefits of digital transformation are shared equitably across society, while also safeguarding against potential harms such as job displacement, income inequality, and loss of privacy.

Investments in digital infrastructure, education, and skills development are essential for equipping workers with the tools and knowledge needed to thrive in the digital economy. Policies that promote entrepreneurship, innovation, and access to capital can foster a vibrant ecosystem of startups and small businesses, driving economic dynamism and job creation. At the same time, regulations must be put in place to protect workers' rights, ensure fair competition, and uphold ethical standards in the use of technology.

In conclusion, the digital age presents both opportunities and challenges for economic transformation, requiring thoughtful and proactive responses from policymakers, businesses, and society as a whole. By harnessing the power of digital technologies for inclusive and sustainable development, we can create an economy that works for everyone, fostering prosperity, innovation, and social progress in the 21st century.

CHAPTER 7

SOCIAL DYNAMICS: CONNECTIVITY AND FRAGMENTATION

In an increasingly interconnected world driven by digital technologies and social media, the dynamics of human interaction are undergoing profound changes. In this chapter, we delve into the complexities of social connectivity and fragmentation, exploring how digital platforms shape our relationships, communities, and identities, and the implications for social cohesion and well-being.

Digital technologies have revolutionized the way we connect and communicate with one another, breaking down geographical barriers and expanding the boundaries of our social networks. Social media platforms such as Facebook, Twitter, and Instagram enable us to stay connected with friends and family, share experiences and opinions, and participate in online communities with like-minded individuals around the globe. Instant messaging apps facilitate real-time communication and collaboration, fostering a sense of intimacy and immediacy in our interactions.

However, the proliferation of digital platforms has also given rise to new forms of social fragmentation and polarization, as algorithms prioritize content that aligns with our preexisting beliefs and preferences, creating echo chambers and filter bubbles that reinforce ideological divides and misinformation. The anonymity and anonymity of online interactions can also lead to the proliferation of hate speech, cyberbullying, and online harassment, undermining trust and civility in digital spaces.

Moreover, the commodification of attention and engagement on social media platforms has led to a culture of hyperconnectivity and constant stimulation, where the pursuit of likes, shares, and followers often takes precedence over genuine human connection and meaningful relationships. The curated nature of social media profiles can also create unrealistic expectations and feelings of inadequacy, leading to negative impacts on mental health and well-being, particularly among young people.

At the same time, digital technologies have also empowered marginalized communities and amplifying voices that have traditionally been silenced or marginalized. Social movements such as #BlackLivesMatter, #MeToo, and Fridays for Future have leveraged digital platforms to mobilize supporters, raise awareness, and effect change on a global scale, demonstrating the potential of technology to drive social progress and advance social justice.

Navigating the complexities of social connectivity and fragmentation requires a nuanced understanding of the role that digital technologies play in shaping our social interactions and relationships. It also requires collective action to promote digital literacy, critical thinking, and empathy in online spaces, empowering individuals to engage constructively with diverse perspectives and navigate the challenges of digital communication responsibly.

Building inclusive and resilient communities in the digital age requires fostering empathy, understanding, and respect for difference, both online and offline. It also requires creating digital environments that prioritize user well-being, privacy, and safety, while also promoting diversity, equity, and inclusion in the design and governance of digital platforms.

In conclusion, the dynamics of social connectivity and fragmentation in the digital age are complex and multifaceted, reflecting the opportunities and challenges of our increasingly interconnected world. By fostering digital literacy, empathy, and inclusivity, we can harness the power of digital technologies to build stronger, more resilient communities and promote social cohesion and well-being for all.

CHAPTER 8

GOVERNANCE IN THE ERA OF TECHNOLOGICAL DISRUPTION

The rapid pace of technological innovation presents unprecedented challenges and opportunities for governance in the 21st century. In this chapter, we examine the evolving role of governments, international organizations, and civil society in navigating the complexities of technological disruption, ensuring accountability, and safeguarding democratic values in an increasingly digital world.

Technological advancements such as artificial intelligence, blockchain, and big data analytics are transforming every aspect of governance, from service delivery and policy-making to citizen engagement and accountability. Governments are leveraging digital technologies to streamline bureaucratic processes, improve transparency and efficiency, and deliver public services more effectively to citizens. E-governance initiatives such as online portals, digital identity systems, and electronic voting platforms are empowering citizens to interact with government institutions more easily and participate in decision-making processes.

However, the digitalization of governance also poses challenges in terms of privacy, security, and accountability. The collection and analysis of vast amounts of data by government agencies raise concerns about surveillance and the potential for abuse of power. Moreover, the use of algorithms in decision-making processes, such as predictive policing and risk assessment tools, has raised questions about fairness, transparency, and bias in automated decision-making.

Ensuring responsible and ethical governance in the era of technological disruption requires robust legal frameworks, regulatory oversight, and accountability mechanisms to protect individual rights and freedoms. Data protection laws, such as the General Data Protection Regulation (GDPR) in the European Union, set standards for the collection, use, and sharing of personal data by government and private sector entities, while also providing mechanisms for individuals to exercise control over their data.

Moreover, governments must invest in digital literacy and skills development to ensure that citizens are equipped to navigate the complexities of the digital world and engage meaningfully in democratic processes. This includes efforts to bridge the digital divide, promote media literacy, and combat misinformation and disinformation online. Civil society plays a crucial role in holding governments accountable for their actions and advocating for transparency, accountability, and respect for human rights in the digital sphere.

At the international level, cooperation and coordination are essential for addressing transnational challenges such as cybercrime, data breaches, and disinformation campaigns. Multilateral organizations such as the United Nations and the European Union play a central role in setting global standards and norms for digital governance, promoting cooperation among member states, and facilitating information sharing and capacity building.

In conclusion, the era of technological disruption presents both opportunities and challenges for governance, requiring adaptive and forward-thinking approaches to ensure that the benefits of digital technologies are equitably distributed and that the rights and freedoms of citizens are protected. By fostering transparency, accountability, and inclusivity in digital governance, we can build more resilient and democratic societies that harness the power of technology for the common good.

CHAPTER
ETHICAL CONSIDERATIONS IN EMERGING TECHNOLOGIES

Emerging technologies, such as artificial intelligence (AI), biotechnology, and nanotechnology, hold tremendous promise for addressing pressing global challenges and improving human welfare. However, alongside their potential benefits, these technologies also raise complex ethical questions and moral dilemmas that must be carefully considered and addressed. In this chapter, we delve into the ethical considerations surrounding emerging technologies, exploring key principles, dilemmas, and frameworks for responsible innovation and governance.

At the heart of ethical considerations in emerging technologies lies the tension between innovation and responsibility, progress and precaution. While technological advancements have the potential to enhance human capabilities, improve quality of life, and address societal challenges, they also pose risks and uncertainties that must be carefully managed. Ethical considerations encompass a wide range of issues, including privacy, safety, fairness, transparency, accountability, and the protection of human rights and dignity.

One of the central ethical dilemmas in emerging technologies is the balance between autonomy and control. Technologies such as AI raise questions about the extent to which humans should delegate decision-making authority to machines, particularly in contexts where the consequences of algorithmic decisions can have profound impacts on individuals' lives and livelihoods. The development of autonomous weapons systems, for example, raises concerns about the delegation of lethal force to machines and the erosion of human responsibility and accountability in warfare.

Another ethical consideration is the principle of justice and fairness in the distribution and access to emerging technologies. The digital divide, for example, exacerbates inequalities in access to information and communication technologies, limiting opportunities for education, economic participation, and social mobility for marginalized communities. Moreover, the potential for emerging technologies to exacerbate existing disparities and create new forms of inequality, such as algorithmic bias and discrimination, underscores the need for proactive measures to promote equity and inclusion in technological innovation and deployment.

Privacy and data protection are also central ethical concerns in the era of big data and ubiquitous surveillance. The collection, analysis, and sharing of personal data by governments and corporations raise questions about consent, transparency, and individual rights to privacy and autonomy. The Cambridge Analytica scandal, in which personal data of millions of Facebook users was harvested without their consent for political advertising purposes, highlighted the risks of data exploitation and the need for stronger privacy regulations and safeguards.

In response to these ethical challenges, policymakers, industry leaders, and civil society organizations are developing ethical frameworks, guidelines, and principles to guide the responsible development and deployment of emerging technologies. Initiatives such as the IEEE Global Initiative on Ethics of Autonomous and Intelligent Systems and the European Union's High-Level Expert Group on AI Ethics provide valuable guidance and recommendations for ensuring that emerging technologies are aligned with ethical principles and values.

Moreover, public engagement and dialogue are essential for fostering ethical awareness, accountability, and trust in emerging technologies. Citizen juries, deliberative forums, and participatory design processes can empower stakeholders to voice their concerns, values, and preferences and shape the direction of technological development in ways that reflect societal values and priorities. Transparency and openness in decision-making processes, as well as mechanisms for accountability and redress, are also critical for building public trust and confidence in emerging technologies.

In conclusion, addressing ethical considerations in emerging technologies requires a multidisciplinary and inclusive approach that engages stakeholders from diverse backgrounds and perspectives. By fostering ethical awareness, accountability, and responsible innovation, we can harness the potential of emerging technologies to advance human welfare and address societal challenges in ways that are equitable, sustainable, and respectful of human rights and dignity.

CHAPTER 10
EDUCATION AND LIFELONG LEARNING IN THE 21ST CENTURY

In the fast-paced and ever-evolving landscape of the 21st century, education and lifelong learning have emerged as indispensable tools for individual empowerment, economic prosperity, and societal resilience. In this chapter, we explore the transformative role of education in preparing individuals for the challenges and opportunities of the digital age, promoting inclusive and equitable access to learning opportunities, and fostering a culture of lifelong learning and innovation.

Education is not merely the acquisition of knowledge and skills but also the cultivation of critical thinking, creativity, and adaptability that are essential for navigating the complexities of the modern world. In an era characterized by rapid technological change and globalization, the ability to learn, unlearn, and relearn is becoming increasingly important for personal and professional success.

However, traditional models of education are often ill-equipped to meet the diverse needs and aspirations of learners in the 21st century. The one-size-fits-all approach to education, with its emphasis on standardized testing and rote memorization, fails to cultivate the creativity, problem-solving, and collaborative skills that are essential for thriving in a knowledge-based economy.

Moreover, persistent disparities in access to quality education, particularly along lines of gender, socioeconomic status, and geography, perpetuate inequalities and limit opportunities for social mobility. Marginalized communities, including girls, children with disabilities, and those living in remote or underserved areas, are often excluded from educational opportunities, depriving them of the chance to fulfil their potential and contribute to the prosperity of their communities and societies.

In response to these challenges, there is growing recognition of the need to reimagine education for the 21st century, with a focus on equity, inclusivity, and lifelong learning. This involves shifting away from traditional models of schooling towards more learner-centred approaches that empower individuals to take ownership of their learning journey and pursue their passions and interests.

Digital technologies have a crucial role to play in transforming education by expanding access to learning resources, personalizing learning experiences, and fostering collaboration and creativity. Online learning platforms, open educational resources, and massive open online courses (MOOCs) offer opportunities for flexible and accessible learning, enabling individuals to learn anytime, anywhere, and at their own pace.

However, realizing the potential of digital technologies in education requires addressing challenges such as the digital divide, digital literacy, and the quality of online learning experiences. Many learners, particularly those from marginalized communities, lack access to reliable internet connectivity, digital devices, and the skills needed to navigate online learning platforms effectively. Moreover, concerns have been raised about the quality and credibility of online educational content and the potential for digital technologies to exacerbate inequalities in learning outcomes.

In addition to expanding access to formal education, there is also a growing recognition of the importance of informal and non-formal learning opportunities in fostering lifelong learning and skills development. Libraries, museums, community centers, and online learning communities offer valuable resources and support for individuals seeking to pursue their interests, develop new skills, and engage with peers and experts in their fields.

Furthermore, there is a need to rethink the role of educators and educational institutions in the 21st century. Teachers are no longer just disseminators of knowledge but also facilitators of learning, mentors, and guides who support and empower learners in their quest for knowledge and understanding. Educational institutions must embrace a culture of innovation, experimentation, and continuous improvement to keep pace with the changing needs and aspirations of learners and society.

In conclusion, education and lifelong learning are essential drivers of individual empowerment, economic prosperity, and societal progress in the 21st century. By embracing innovation, equity, and inclusivity in education, we can unlock the full potential of every individual and build a future where learning is a lifelong journey of discovery, growth, and fulfilment.

CHAPTER 11

URBANIZATION AND SUSTAINABLE CITIES

The 21st century has witnessed unprecedented urbanization, with more than half of the world's population now living in cities. This trend is expected to continue in the coming decades, posing both challenges and opportunities for sustainable development. In this chapter, we explore the dynamics of urbanization, the key drivers of urban growth, and strategies for building sustainable and resilient cities that promote prosperity, equity, and environmental stewardship.

Urbanization is driven by a combination of factors, including population growth, rural-to-urban migration, and economic development. Cities offer opportunities for employment, education, healthcare, and cultural enrichment, attracting people from rural areas in search of a better quality of life and economic opportunities. However, rapid urbanization also strains infrastructure, services, and resources, leading to congestion, pollution, and social inequalities.

One of the key challenges of urbanization is ensuring that cities are inclusive and equitable, providing opportunities and services for all residents, regardless of their income, gender, ethnicity, or background. In many cities, marginalized communities such as slum dwellers, informal workers, and migrants face barriers to accessing basic services such as housing, water, sanitation, and healthcare, perpetuating cycles of poverty and exclusion.

Moreover, urbanization places immense pressure on natural resources and ecosystems, exacerbating environmental degradation and climate change. Cities are major consumers of energy and resources, accounting for a significant share of global greenhouse gas emissions and ecological footprint. Unplanned urban expansion, deforestation, and pollution degrade air and water quality, threaten biodiversity, and increase the vulnerability of cities to natural disasters and climate-related hazards.

In response to these challenges, there is growing recognition of the need to promote sustainable urban development, characterized by compact, connected, and resilient cities that balance economic growth with environmental sustainability and social inclusion. Sustainable cities prioritize investments in public transportation, affordable housing, green spaces, and renewable energy infrastructure, reducing dependency on private vehicles, promoting active transportation, and improving quality of life for residents.

Smart city technologies, such as IoT sensors, data analytics, and digital platforms, offer opportunities for enhancing the efficiency, resilience, and liveability of urban environments. These technologies enable cities to optimize resource use, improve service delivery, and empower citizens to participate in decision-making processes. However, it is essential to ensure that smart city initiatives are inclusive, transparent, and respectful of privacy rights and data security concerns.

Furthermore, sustainable urban development requires integrated and participatory approaches that engage stakeholders from government, civil society, the private sector, and local communities. Urban planning and governance must be guided by principles of transparency, accountability, and democratic participation, ensuring that the needs and aspirations of all residents are taken into account in decision-making processes.

In conclusion, urbanization presents both challenges and opportunities for sustainable development, requiring innovative and collaborative solutions to build cities that are inclusive, resilient, and environmentally sustainable. By embracing principles of equity, efficiency, and environmental stewardship, we can create cities that provide opportunities for all residents to thrive, now and in the future.

CHAPTER 12

RESILIENCE IN THE FACE OF GLOBAL CHALLENGES

In an era defined by interconnectedness and rapid change, building resilience has become essential for individuals, communities, and societies to withstand and adapt to a wide range of global challenges. In this chapter, we explore the concept of resilience, its importance in addressing complex and dynamic threats, and strategies for fostering resilience at the individual, community, and global levels.

Resilience can be defined as the ability to bounce back from adversity, to adapt to change, and to thrive in the face of challenges. It encompasses physical, psychological, social, and economic dimensions, enabling individuals and communities to withstand shocks and stresses, recover from setbacks, and emerge stronger and more resourceful.

At the individual level, resilience involves cultivating inner strength, coping skills, and adaptive strategies to navigate life's ups and downs. This includes developing self-awareness, emotional intelligence, and problem-solving abilities, as well as fostering supportive relationships and social networks that provide emotional and practical support during difficult times.

Building resilience at the community level requires fostering social cohesion, solidarity, and collective action to address shared challenges and promote mutual aid and support. This involves investing in social capital, community infrastructure, and disaster preparedness measures that enhance the ability of communities to respond effectively to crises and emergencies.

Moreover, resilience at the global level requires fostering cooperation, collaboration, and solidarity among nations and international organizations to address transnational threats such as climate change, pandemics, and geopolitical instability. This includes strengthening global governance mechanisms, promoting multilateralism, and investing in international development and humanitarian assistance to build resilience in vulnerable regions and populations.

In recent years, the COVID-19 pandemic has highlighted the importance of resilience in responding to global crises. Countries and communities that were able to adapt quickly, mobilize resources, and work together effectively have fared better in mitigating the impacts of the pandemic and protecting the health and well-being of their citizens.

However, the pandemic has also exposed vulnerabilities and inequalities within and between countries, underscoring the need for a more inclusive and equitable approach to resilience-building. This includes addressing structural inequalities, investing in social safety nets, and strengthening healthcare systems to ensure that all individuals and communities have the resources and support they need to thrive.

In conclusion, building resilience is essential for addressing the complex and interconnected challenges of the 21st century. By fostering resilience at the individual, community, and global levels, we can adapt to change, withstand adversity, and create a more sustainable and equitable world for future generations.

CHAPTER 13

CULTIVATING GLOBAL CITIZENSHIP IN AN INTERCONNECTED WORLD

In an increasingly interconnected and interdependent world, the concept of global citizenship has gained prominence as a guiding principle for addressing shared challenges and promoting collective action for the common good. In this chapter, we explore the meaning of global citizenship, its significance in the context of globalization, and strategies for cultivating a sense of global responsibility and solidarity among individuals and communities.

Global citizenship encompasses a sense of belonging to a broader community beyond national boundaries, recognizing the interconnectedness of our world and the shared humanity that unites us. It is grounded in values of respect, empathy, and solidarity, and entails a commitment to promoting justice, equity, and sustainability at local, national, and global levels. Global citizens are mindful of the impact of their actions on others and strive to contribute positively to the well-being of people and the planet.

One of the key principles of global citizenship is the recognition of the inherent dignity and rights of all individuals, regardless of their nationality, ethnicity, religion, or socioeconomic status. Global citizens advocate for human rights, social justice, and equality, and work to address systemic injustices and inequalities that perpetuate poverty, discrimination, and marginalization. They are active agents of positive change in their communities, advocating for inclusive policies and practices that uphold the rights and dignity of all people.

Moreover, global citizenship involves fostering cross-cultural understanding, appreciation, and respect for diversity. In an increasingly diverse and multicultural world, global citizens recognize the value of cultural exchange and dialogue in building bridges of understanding and promoting peace and harmony. They embrace cultural differences as a source of strength and enrichment, rather than a source of division or conflict, and seek opportunities to learn from and collaborate with people from different backgrounds and perspectives.

Education plays a crucial role in cultivating global citizenship by equipping individuals with the knowledge, skills, and attitudes needed to engage critically and constructively with global issues and perspectives. Global citizenship education emphasizes interdisciplinary learning, critical thinking, and active citizenship, empowering students to become informed, responsible, and ethical global citizens. It promotes values such as empathy, tolerance, and respect for diversity, and provides opportunities for students to explore global challenges and solutions through real-world experiences and service-learning projects.

Beyond formal education, fostering global citizenship requires creating opportunities for meaningful engagement and participation in global issues and initiatives. Civil society organizations, grassroots movements, and international institutions play a crucial role in providing platforms for dialogue, collaboration, and collective action on issues such as climate change, human rights, and global health. Digital technologies also offer opportunities for global engagement and activism, enabling individuals to connect, organize, and mobilize across borders to address shared challenges and promote positive change.

In conclusion, cultivating global citizenship is essential for building a more just, peaceful, and sustainable world in the 21st century.

By embracing the principles of global citizenship—respect for human rights, appreciation of diversity, and commitment to social justice and sustainability—we can harness the power of collective action and solidarity to address global challenges and create a brighter future for all.

CHAPTER 14

THE FUTURE OF WORK IN THE DIGITAL ECONOMY

The digital economy is reshaping the nature of work, transforming industries, occupations, and employment relationships in profound ways. In this chapter, we explore the future of work in the digital age, examining the impact of automation, artificial intelligence, and the gig economy on employment trends, skills requirements, and labour market dynamics, as well as strategies for ensuring inclusive and sustainable work opportunities for all.

Advancements in automation and artificial intelligence are revolutionizing the way work is performed, augmenting human capabilities, and reshaping the division of labour between humans and machines. Routine and repetitive tasks are increasingly being automated, while jobs that require creativity, problem-solving, and emotional intelligence are becoming more valued. This shift is driving demand for new skills and competencies, such as digital literacy, critical thinking, and adaptability, while also creating opportunities for innovation and entrepreneurship.

The rise of the gig economy, characterized by short-term contracts, freelance work, and platform-based employment, is also transforming the nature of work and employment relationships. Digital platforms such as Uber, Airbnb, and Upwork have democratized access to work opportunities, enabling individuals to monetize their skills and assets on a flexible basis. While the gig economy offers benefits such as flexibility and autonomy, it also raises concerns about job insecurity, income volatility, and lack of social protections for workers.

Moreover, the COVID-19 pandemic has accelerated trends such as remote work and digitalization, prompting organizations to rethink traditional models of work and embrace remote and hybrid work arrangements. Remote work offers benefits such as flexibility, cost savings, and access to a global talent pool, but it also presents challenges in terms of maintaining productivity, collaboration, and work-life balance, particularly for vulnerable groups such as women, caregivers, and low-income workers.

Addressing the challenges and opportunities of the future of work requires a comprehensive and integrated approach that addresses both technological and social dimensions. On the technological front, investments in digital infrastructure, skills development, and innovation are needed to ensure that workers are equipped to thrive in the digital economy. This includes efforts to close the digital divide, promote digital literacy, and provide training and reskilling opportunities for workers whose jobs are at risk of automation.

On the social front, there is a need to strengthen labour protections, social safety nets, and access to lifelong learning and training opportunities to ensure that all workers can benefit from the opportunities of the digital economy. This includes measures such as portable benefits, universal basic income, and lifelong learning accounts that provide workers with financial security and support their ongoing skills development and career advancement.

Furthermore, there is a need to reimagine the social contract between employers, workers, and society to ensure that the benefits of technological progress are shared equitably and that workers have a voice in shaping the future of work. This may involve new forms of collective bargaining, worker representation, and stakeholder engagement that empower workers to advocate for their rights and interests in the digital economy.

In conclusion, the future of work in the digital economy offers both opportunities and challenges for individuals, communities, and societies. By embracing innovation, investing in human capital, and fostering inclusive and sustainable work opportunities, we can create a future of work that is fair, inclusive, and equitable for all.

CHAPTER 15
ENVIRONMENTAL CONSERVATION AND SUSTAINABLE DEVELOPMENT

Environmental conservation and sustainable development are paramount in ensuring the well-being of current and future generations and preserving the integrity of the planet's ecosystems. In this chapter, we delve into the importance of environmental conservation, the challenges posed by environmental degradation, and strategies for achieving sustainable development goals while safeguarding the environment.

Environmental conservation encompasses a range of practices and policies aimed at protecting natural resources, biodiversity, and ecosystems from degradation and depletion. It involves efforts to preserve habitats, conserve endangered species, and reduce pollution and waste generation. Conservation initiatives also seek to promote sustainable land use, water management, and energy production to minimize the environmental footprint of human activities.

However, environmental conservation faces numerous challenges, including deforestation, habitat destruction, pollution, climate change, and resource depletion. Human activities, such as industrialization, urbanization, and intensive agriculture, have accelerated environmental degradation, threatened the stability and resilience of ecosystems and jeopardized the provision of ecosystem services essential for human well-being.

Climate change, in particular, poses a significant threat to the environment and human societies, exacerbating natural disasters, disrupting ecosystems, and exacerbating social inequalities. Rising temperatures, changing precipitation patterns, and extreme weather events are already having profound impacts on agriculture, water resources, and public health, disproportionately affecting vulnerable communities and exacerbating food insecurity, displacement, and conflict.

In response to these challenges, there is growing recognition of the need to transition towards more sustainable and resilient development pathways that balance economic growth with environmental protection and social equity. Sustainable development aims to meet the needs of the present without compromising the ability of future generations to meet their own needs, ensuring a harmonious balance between human activities and the natural environment.

Achieving sustainable development requires integrated and participatory approaches that address social, economic, and environmental dimensions of development. This involves promoting sustainable consumption and production patterns, investing in renewable energy, and adopting green technologies and practices that minimize environmental impact and promote resource efficiency.

Furthermore, sustainable development requires international cooperation and solidarity to address transboundary environmental challenges and promote global sustainability. Multilateral agreements such as the Paris Agreement on climate change and the Convention on Biological Diversity provide frameworks for collective action and collaboration to tackle environmental issues on a global scale. However, achieving consensus and implementing effective policies requires political will, commitment, and cooperation among nations, civil society, and the private sector.

In conclusion, environmental conservation and sustainable development are essential for ensuring the long-term health and prosperity of people and the planet. By embracing principles of sustainability, stewardship, and intergenerational equity, we can create a future where human activities are in harmony with nature, and all people can thrive in a healthy and resilient environment.

CONCLUSION: NAVIGATING THE CHALLENGES AND OPPORTUNITIES OF THE 21ST CENTURY

As we reach the conclusion of this exploration into the future of humanity in the 21st century, it becomes evident that we are at a pivotal moment in history. The rapid pace of technological advancement, environmental change, and globalization presents both unprecedented challenges and opportunities for individuals, communities, and societies around the world.

Throughout this book, we have examined a wide range of topics, from technological transformations and global challenges to social dynamics and environmental conservation, highlighting the complexities and interconnectedness of the issues facing humanity in the 21st century. We have explored the transformative power of digital technologies, the importance of social cohesion and inclusion, and the urgent need for sustainable development and environmental stewardship.

In the face of these challenges, it is clear that no single solution or approach will suffice. Addressing the multifaceted challenges of the 21st century requires collective action, collaboration, and innovation across all sectors of society. It requires reimagining our systems, institutions, and behaviours to ensure that they are equitable, inclusive, and sustainable for future generations.

As we move forward into an uncertain future, it is essential to embrace the principles of resilience, adaptability, and empathy that are central to human flourishing. We must cultivate a sense of global citizenship, recognizing our shared humanity and interconnectedness, and working together to address the pressing challenges of our time.

By harnessing the power of technology for good, fostering social cohesion and inclusion, and promoting environmental conservation and sustainable development, we can create a future that is more just, equitable, and resilient for all. It will require bold leadership, innovative thinking, and collective action, but by working together, we can build a brighter future for generations to come.

As we embark on this journey into the future, let us remember that the choices we make today will shape the world of tomorrow. Let us strive to leave a legacy of hope, compassion, and stewardship for the planet and all its inhabitants. Together, we can navigate the challenges and opportunities of the 21st century and build a future that reflects our shared values and aspirations for a better world.

Thank you for joining us on this journey.

www.ingramcontent.com/pod-product-compliance
Lightning Source LLC
Chambersburg PA
CBHW081450250726

48662CB00009B/3020